THE SEVEN WONDERS

OF THE

ANCIENT WORLD

Diana Bentley

OXFORD
UNIVERSITY PRESS

In Association with the British Museum

CONTENTS

© 2001 Diana Bentley

First published in 2001 by The British Museum Press, a division of The British Museum Company Ltd
46 Bloomsbury Street, London, WC1B 3QQ

Library of Congress Cataloging-in-Publication data is available.

ISBN 0-19-521914-7 trade ed.; ISBN 0-19-521913-9 lib. ed.

Designed and typeset in Leawood by Carla Turchini
The Seven Wonders and the front cover illustration were drawn by Sarah Warburton
Printed and bound in Slovenia by Preševnova družba, Ljubljana

The Seven Wonders of the Ancient World

Two centuries before the birth of Jesus Christ, Antipater, a Greek poet in the Palestinian city of Sidon, listed seven spectacular monuments created by humans. These wonders astonished all who saw them for their sheer size and splendor. Antipater's list included the Pyramids of Giza, the Statue of Zeus at Olympia, the Walls and Hanging Gardens of Babylon, the Temple of Artemis at Ephesus, the Colossus of Rhodes, and the Mausoleum at Halicarnassus.

The idea of having a list of wonders became popular and other people created their own lists. By the time of the Renaissance in Europe, some 1,500 years after Antipater, the list of the Seven Wonders of the Ancient World had become fixed. It included six of the wonders on Antipater's list, but instead of the Walls of Babylon, the seventh wonder became the Lighthouse at Alexandria in Egypt.

All these monuments showed how people in past ages had mastered technical problems and the ability to complete large-scale projects without any of the benefits of modern technology. The Seven Wonders displayed the imagination and boldness of their builders, and still remind us of the talent humans have to create artistic works of great beauty. Most of the Seven Wonders also became models for other famous structures in later history.

In time, most of the Seven Wonders of the Ancient World were destroyed by people or by the forces of nature. Some were gradually buried and their exact whereabouts were forgotten. Today only the Pyramids at Giza are still standing, but the development of archaeology (the study of ancient things) over the last 200 years has helped us to find out more about the others. Archaeologists have uncovered the remains of some of the Seven Wonders and their discoveries have helped to show us just how extraordinary these monuments were.

The Pyramids at Giza

The Pyramids at Giza in Egypt are the oldest of the Seven Wonders of the Ancient World and they are also the only ones still standing. No one knows exactly how these great tombs were built, but for over 4,000 years the Great Pyramid of Khufu was the tallest building in the world.

The civilization of ancient Egypt is one of the oldest in the world. People began to live along the fertile banks of the Nile River about 7,000 years ago. About 2,000 years later, Egypt became one country, ruled by a single king. The ancient Egyptians created marvelous works of art, built towering temples, and developed their own religion. The pyramids are among their most lasting and beautiful monuments. These massive structures are square at the bottom with four triangular sides. The Egyptians worshipped a sun god, Re, and they may have chosen the pyramid shape to represent the rays of the sun pouring down to earth, or perhaps they thought the dead king buried in the pyramid could use its sloping sides as a staircase to climb to the gods in the sky.

The Power of the Afterlife

The Egyptians believed that after death people went to another world where their bodies would live again, so they preserved dead bodies by a process called mummification. The bodies were embalmed, wrapped in bandages and protected in tombs which were meant to last for ever. Pyramids were built as royal tombs to house the bodies of kings, or "pharaohs," who were buried with magical equipment to help them in the next life.

Pyramids

Pyramids were built in the north of Egypt between 2670 and 1899 BC, mainly on the west bank of the Nile. At first they had a stepped shape, but later pyramids had smooth sides covered with white limestone. The pyramids of ancient Egypt are the most famous, but stepped pyramids were also built by people in other parts of the world, such as Mesopotamia and Central America. These were built later than the Egyptian pyramids and their purpose was different—for example, some included temples for human sacrifice.

The Miracle of Giza

In about 2560 BC the Egyptian king Khufu, who is sometimes known by his Greek name Cheops, built a pyramid at Giza in the desert near Egypt's modern capital, Cairo. Two smaller pyramids were later built nearby for Khufu's successors, Khafre and Menkaure. These three pyramids are the finest examples of pyramid building in Egypt and they are also the largest. They were surrounded by temples where priests could make offerings to the dead kings, and by the smaller tombs of the royal family and servants.

Khufu's pyramid is called the Great Pyramid and it is well named. The Greek historian Herodotus believed that it took about twenty years to build. Nearly two and a half million blocks of stone were used, many weighing about 2.25 tons each. The Great Pyramid stands 481 feet (145.75 meters) high, even though part of its top is now missing, and covers a massive area of 13.1 acres (5.37 hectares). It is so big that Westminster Abbey and St. Paul's in London, St. Peters in Rome, and the cathedrals of Florence and Milan could all fit inside it.

King Khufu reigned for twenty-three years but, despite the immense size of his pyramid, the only image we have of him is a tiny ivory statue.

Ivory statue of Khufu, the builder of the Great Pyramid.

A Mighty Task

Exactly how the pyramids were built is still a mystery. The ancient Egyptians used rollers and levers but had no tools like the pulley to help them lift the massive blocks of stone. We know that the builders began by making the ground level and then matched the four sides of the pyramids to face north, south, east, and west. The sides were measured very accurately with rope. In Khufu's Great Pyramid, the difference in length between the longest and shortest sides is only about 8 in. (20 cm).

Stones were cut in quarries across the Nile River, and further south, and taken by boat to the site, where they were shaped and dragged on log rollers from the river to the building area. Different ideas exist about how they were raised and fitted into place. Herodotus says that the Egyptians used machines made of wooden planks, while others believe that the stones were taken on sleds or rollers up a ramp that spiralled round the pyramid. Archaeologists have found the remains of ramps near the pyramids.

Herodotus said the pyramids were built by slaves, but he was wrong. Free Egyptian men worked on them for a few months each year, especially when the Nile River flooded the land and no farming could be done. Pyramid building was one of man's first attempts at building on a massive scale and it demanded great skill and organization. Any monument built now which lasted as long as the Great Pyramid would still be standing in the year 6562!

> "These pyramids far excel all other works throughout Egypt, not only in the greatness and costs of the building but in the excellency of the workmanship."
> *Diodorus of Sicily*

Inside the Great Pyramid

The entrance to a pyramid was usually on its north side so that it faced the polar star, which was important in Egypt's religion. Like most pyramids the Great Pyramid had a chamber inside where the king was buried. A passage called the Grand Gallery slopes up 153 feet (47 meters) into the center to the burial chamber, called the "King's Chamber." Khufu's stone sarcophagus (coffin), carved from one massive piece of granite, lies inside the chamber. Two narrow passages slope upward from the chamber to the outer surface of the pyramid. The Egyptians believed the dead king could see the sun god's daily journey across the sky through these shafts. When the king was buried, workers inside sealed the entrance passage with a great stone, then escaped by a secret passageway.

Raided by Tomb Robbers

Unfortunately, tomb robbers quickly found ways to break inside the pyramids; the Great Pyramid was long ago robbed of its treasures, and Khufu's mummified body disappeared. Building gigantic pyramids was also a great burden on the Egyptian people as it involved thousands of workers and much time and money. The Egyptians later remembered King Khufu as a great tyrant and no one in Egypt ever built such a large pyramid again. From about 1567 BC the Egyptians stopped building pyramids altogether, and Egyptian kings and queens were buried in hidden underground tombs in the Valleys of the Kings and Queens near modern Luxor. The pyramids at Giza remained standing, but their appearance changed. In the fourteenth century, most of their limestone covering was taken away and used for buildings in Cairo. Only King Khafre's pyramid still has some limestone on top.

The pyramids of Giza rise up dramatically from the desert.

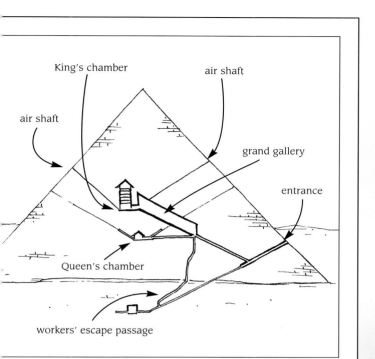

King's chamber

air shaft

air shaft

grand gallery

entrance

Queen's chamber

workers' escape passage

Pyramids Today

There were as many as 90 pyramids in ancient Egypt. Most of the major ones have now been thoroughly studied, but new discoveries are still being made. In 1954 a large wooden boat owned by Khufu was found buried in a pit near the Great Pyramid. Archaeologists are still studying the tombs surrounding the pyramids at Giza.

Pyramids have continued to fascinate us. Ever since ancient times people have made their own tombs look like copies of Egyptian pyramids or temples. New pyramids are even being built today, though not as tombs. One extraordinary example is made of glass and stands outside the Louvre Museum in Paris.

The spectacular glass pyramid at the Louvre Museum, Paris.

The Valley of the Kings.

The Statue of Zeus at Olympia

The first Olympic Games were athletic contests held in ancient Greece to honor Zeus, the mighty king of the Greek gods. For over 800 years people marveled at the colossal statue of the god which stood in the great temple of Zeus at Olympia. It was made by Pheidias, one of the most brilliant sculptors of the ancient world. This gigantic statue was made from gold, ivory, and precious stones, and its size and beauty dazzled all who saw it.

Olympia lies on a fertile plain in a part of southern Greece called the Peloponnese. It was a place of worship from about 1000 BC. The god Zeus is said to have thrown a thunderbolt which struck the earth there and marked it as a sacred spot. Olympia became one of the most important centers of the worship of Zeus in the Greek world and attracted many pilgrims.

Sculpture in Greece

Sculpture in Greece was a highly prized art and graceful and dramatic sculptures were made to decorate buildings or to stand in public places. These statues represented gods and heroes and great events, or men and women of ideal beauty. At first statues were made of wood and clay but later marble and metals like bronze became more popular. The historian Pliny the Elder says there were 3,000 statues of gods and athletes at Olympia.

The Olympic Games

The Greeks believed that the Olympic games started in 776 BC. At first, only running races were held, but many exciting sports were added later, including chariot races, wrestling, and boxing. In time a great sacred and sporting complex developed at Olympia, with many temples and other religious buildings. There were also facilities for the games: a stadium for foot races, a gymnasium, and a course for horse races called a "hippodrome." The games were held every four years and only people of Greek blood could take part. On the middle day of the games, 100 oxen were slaughtered and burned as a sacrifice to Zeus.

In AD 391 the Roman emperor Theodosius I stopped the Games and closed the temples of Olympia because he felt they were not Christian. The games did not begin again until 1896.

The Home of Zeus

The temple for Zeus at Olympia was built between about 468 and 456 BC. The architect was a man called Libon who designed the temple in the 'Doric' style, which was plain but very impressive. Thirty-four Doric columns surrounded the temple, which was magnificently adorned. At each end a triangular section of the roof called the 'pediment' was filled with sculptures, and carvings showing tales from Greek legends ran around the temple. Patterns in red, blue and gold were painted on the tops of columns. The sculptures too were brightly painted and must have looked very much alive.

> "And we will sing in loftiest strain,
> The contest of Olympia's plain."
> *Pindar, Greek poet*

Above: **A Greek pot showing athletes in a running race.**

Right: **A modern model of the site of Olympia, showing the temple of Zeus.**

9

Pheidias the Sculptor

Shortly after the temple was built Pheidias (c. 500-432 BC), a sculptor of Athens, was chosen to make a great statue of Zeus to stand inside it. Pheidias trained as a sculptor with the great artists of Greece, and was the first to make "chryselephantine" statues (statues made of gold and ivory). Pheidias had already made two great statues of the goddess Athena for Athens. Also, the dramatic sculptures which decorated the Parthenon in Athens were probably carved under his direction. None of his work survives today, but he is mainly remembered for his statue of Zeus in Olympia.

The Fate of the Statue

The statue had stood in the temple for 450 years when the Roman emperor Caligula tried to take it back to Rome. According to legend, the statue let out a mighty laugh, and Caligula's workmen fled in terror.

After the emperor Theodosius I ended the Games, Olympia fell into disrepair. In AD 425 fire destroyed the Temple of Zeus. In the fourth century AD two earthquakes shattered Olympia and did much damage, then two nearby rivers flooded the site. Olympia became covered with soil and was forgotten.

The exact fate of the great statue is uncertain. Some say it was destroyed in the temple fire. Others say it was taken to Constantinople, now called Istanbul, in Turkey and was burned in a fire in AD 462.

A Dazzling Giant

A small bronze statuette of Zeus.

We know from several sources what the statue looked like. Several Greek coins show a gigantic, seated figure of Zeus which was probably the statue at Olympia. The Greek traveler Pausanias visited Olympia in the second century AD and described the statue in his writings. He said the god was seated on a throne richly decorated with gold, ebony, and precious stones. He wore a crown of olive leaves made of green enameled gold. In his right hand he held a figure of Nike, the goddess of victory. In his left hand, he held a scepter topped with a sculptured eagle. The statue is said to have stood about 40 feet (13 meters) high—that is as tall as a three- or four-story building.

Making the Statue

Pheidias made the statue on a wooden frame. Pieces of ivory were shaped and fitted to the frame to look like flesh, and this was apparently done so well that the joins could not be seen. The god's clothes and ornaments were made of gold. The statue was placed in the innermost part of the temple, which only priests could enter. It was said that when Pheidias finished the statue, he asked Zeus for a sign of approval, and immediately a bolt of lightning struck the floor in front of the statue. Afterward the spot was marked with a bronze vase. The colossal statue astonished all who saw it, not only for its beauty, but because it perfectly showed the massive power and majesty of the god.

The Legacy of Olympia

Olympia lay in ruins for over 1,000 years until it was discovered in 1766 by an Englishman, Richard Chandler. In 1829 French archaeologists began investigating Olympia and found some sculptures. German archaeologists began excavations there in 1875. Many of Olympia's buildings and the foundations of the temple of Zeus were uncovered, and pieces of sculpture, coins, and pottery were found.

In 1958, archaeologists discovered some remains of the workshop of Pheidias, where they found discarded tools and molds that had been used to make the statue. There was even a cup which had the words "I belong to Pheidias" scratched on it.

Olympia left its mark on the world. People have never tired of making huge statues of gods and famous people, and the Olympic Games are again the most exciting sporting event in the world. They remind us of the Olympia of old and its glorious statue.

This cup is inscribed on the bottom "I belong to Pheidias."

A gigantic statue of Abraham Lincoln, in the Lincoln memorial, Washington, D.C.

Below: **The modern Games, and the site of Olympia today.**

These bronze tools were found during the excavation of Pheidias's workshop at Olympia.

The Hanging Gardens of Babylon

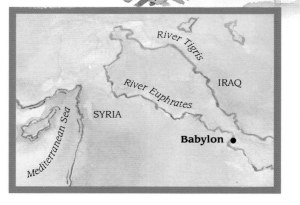

The Hanging Gardens of Babylon are the most mysterious of all the Seven Wonders of the Ancient World. Little was written about them and not a trace of them remains today. The gardens were said to have been built high above the ground on terraces, and people who saw them marveled at their beauty and at the extraordinary skill shown by those who created them.

River Tigris

River Euphrates

IRAQ

SYRIA

Babylon ●

Mediterranean Sea

One of the world's first major civilizations arose between the Tigris and Euphrates rivers in the Near East. The Greeks and Romans called the area Mesopotamia, which means "the land between the rivers." This area is now modern Iraq. The people of Mesopotamia—the Sumerians, the Assyrians, and the Babylonians—pioneered farming, art, science, literature, and architecture, and developed cuneiform, one of the earliest forms of writing. They could also be warlike: the Assyrian army was known for its cruelty.

The city of Babylon, which lay on a broad, fertile plain, became the capital of the kingdom of Babylonia. In 689 BC it was destroyed by the Assyrian king, Sennacherib, but it rose again after 625 BC, when King Nabopolessar seized the city. He and his son, Nebuchadnezzar II, founded a new Babylonian empire and turned Babylon into the most splendid city of its time.

The reconstructed Ishtar Gate.

A Vigorous King

Nebuchadnezzar II (604–562 BC) was a great soldier and he became the master of a vast empire. In 586 BC he captured Jerusalem, destroyed its temple and took the Jews as captives to Babylon. Nebuchadnezzar was determined to make Babylon a dazzling capital. He built immense double walls around the city which soared 70 feet (21 meters) into the air. It was said that they were so wide that two four-horse chariots could pass each other driving along the top. Inside the walls lay a vast area of fields, gardens and houses.

Nebuchadnezzar built magnificent palaces and monuments in Babylon. There was little stone or timber in the area so his buildings were mostly made of bricks. Nebuchadnezzar rebuilt the temple of Marduk, the most important god worshipped by the Babylonians. The temple included a ziggurat, which looked like a stepped pyramid and may have been the origin of the Tower of Babel mentioned in the Bible. A great street, called the Processional Way, led from the mighty Ishtar Gate in the city walls to the temple. Brightly colored tiles showing lions, dragons, and bulls decorated the gate and walls.

The Gardens of Mesopotamia

The Mesopotamians were some of the first people in the world to settle in one place to grow crops and raise animals. They became experts at managing their rivers and built canals to water their farmlands. Plantations of palm trees may have been their first gardens. They later planted gardens of vegetables and grew fruit trees, spices for cooking, and herbs used in medicine.

Mesopotamian kings delighted in exotic plants and flowers, and it became a tradition to plant royal gardens. Assurnasirpal II, king of Assyria from 883–859 BC, planted gardens near the Tigris River.

Sennacherib, a later king of Assyria, built a huge garden near his palace in Nineveh with plants from many countries. The king wrote that he brought water to the garden by an aqueduct. His garden is shown on a carved stone sculpture in the British Museum.

The Hanging Gardens

The kings of Babylon wrote boastfully about what they built but, strangely, there are no Babylonian records that mention the Hanging Gardens. One Greek writer, Berossus, a priest in Babylon, wrote that Nebuchadnezzar had terraces in his palace on which gardens were planted. A traditional story is that the king built the gardens to please his wife, Amitiya, a Persian princess who was homesick for the charming gardens of her home.

Water may have been raised to the terraces by a mechanism called an Archimedes screw. A spiral screw inside a hollow pipe lifts water from the lower container to the higher as it is rotated.

"The paths are full of scent: the waterfalls (sparkle) like the stars of heaven in the garden of pleasure. The pomegranate trees ... enrich the breezes in this garden of delight."
Assurnasirpal II

Left: **A stone carving of Sennacherib's garden.**

Right: **Statue of Assurnasirpal II.**

Decline Foretold

Two great Jewish prophets, Isaiah and Jeremiah, predicted that Babylon would decline and be abandoned. Their words were proved true when, in 538 BC, the Persian king Cyrus captured Babylon, and 3,000 years of Mesopotamian power ended. Babylon became part of the massive Persian empire. The Greek general Alexander the Great later entered the city, where he died in 323 BC in one of Nebuchadnezzar's palaces. By then Babylon was beginning to decline. By the sixth century AD, it was abandoned, and its bricks were used for building in towns nearby. From the twelfth century onward, travelers passing through found Babylon in ruins and full of snakes and scorpions.

Building the Gardens

It was said that the gardens were built in stepped terraces which rose high into the air until they reached the top of the city walls. The terraces were supported by arches and a massive outer wall. There were rooms underneath the arches, where people could walk in the cool air and relax. The gardens did indeed seem to "hang" in the air. Steps led from one terrace to another, and water from the Euphrates River was drawn up the terraces, though no one knows exactly how. The terraces were covered with asphalt to stop water seeping through, and soil was laid on top.

Treasures Refound

In the early nineteenth century, an Englishman who lived in Baghdad, Claudius Rich, explored the crumbling remains of Babylon. The German archaeologist Robert Koldewey began excavating Babylon in 1899 and continued until 1912. The Processional Way and the Ishtar Gate were uncovered and are now in the Pergamon Museum in Berlin. Today the ruins of Babylon cover some 344 acres (850 hectares), but nobody has ever found any definite remains of the gardens.

The Hanging Gardens remain a tantalizing mystery, but the legend of the gardens has remained popular over the centuries. People have never tired of creating beautiful gardens. In the seventeenth-century, Count Carlo Borromeo laid out a splendid garden on an Italian island in Lake Maggiore called the Isola Bella. His garden contained flower-laden terraces and may have looked a little bit like the Hanging Gardens.

Above: **Isola Bella.**

Love of gardens survives to this day. Our word "paradise" comes from a Near Eastern word that originally meant "park" or "garden." People have often imagined paradise as a beautiful garden of great happiness, like the Garden of Eden described in the Bible.

"Therefore the wild beasts of the desert ... shall dwell there ... it shall be no more inhabited forever: neither shall it be dwelt in from generation to generation."
Isaiah 13:20

Left: **A stela (memorial stone) from the temple of Marduk in Babylon, showing a priest and his son.**

Below: **The ruins of Babylon today.**

The Temple of Artemis at Ephesus

Many great temples were built throughout the ancient Greek world, but the temple of the goddess Artemis in Ephesus was the largest and most beautiful of them all. It became famous far and wide as a place of pilgrimage and refuge, and as a financial center.

The city of Ephesus, which lay in Asia Minor (modern Turkey) near the sea at the mouth of the Cayster River, was one of the great cities of the ancient world. According to legend, it was founded around 1000 BC by Androclus, a son of the king of Athens. From the beginning Ephesus was a religious center where the goddess Artemis was worshiped, and it also became an important center for trade with countries further to the east. Many famous people visited the city. The apostle St. Paul lived there for two years in the first century AD. St. John also lived in Ephesus and wrote his gospel there.

The Goddess Artemis

Artemis was the Greek goddess of the hunt, and in Greek art she appears with a bow and arrow and a hunting dog. People in Asia Minor also saw Artemis as a mother goddess, and statues showed her with many breasts, and with animals on her clothes. She was a symbol of motherhood and of the richness of the earth. Artemis was also believed to be bold and brave, and there are many stories about her. The Ephesians continued to worship Artemis until the fourth century AD.

Artemis, shown as a mother goddess.

"Whoever examines (the temple) would believe that the gods had left their immortal regions and come down and lived on earth...."
Philo of Byzantium

Greek Temples

In ancient Greece, temples were not places where people gathered to worship, like churches, mosques and temples today. Greek temples were designed to be the house of a god, where cult statues of the god were kept. Sacrifices of animals were offered to the gods at an altar outside the temple. People showed pride in their city and gained fame for themselves by paying for the building of grand temples.

Greek temples were famous for their beautiful, elegant design. They usually stood on a stone platform and were surrounded by columns which supported the roof.

The Parthenon temple in Athens.

17

The Artemisium

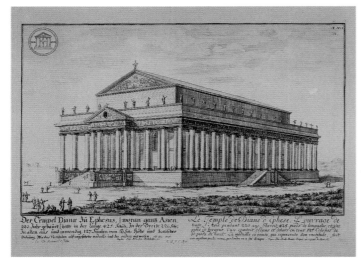

A 16th-century engraving of the temple of Artemis.

In the seventh and sixth centuries BC there was an altar to Artemis at Ephesus. Three temples were built for the goddess, but each was destroyed. In about 550 BC a fourth great temple for Artemis was begun, and Croesus, the wealthy king of a nearby land called Lydia, helped to pay for it. The architects of this temple, called the Artemisium, were Chersiphron and his son Metegenes of Crete. The Artemisium, which took many years to build, was known for its rich decoration. Some of the greatest sculptors of the time, including Pheidias, the sculptor of the statue of Zeus at Olympia, made statues for the altar and the temple. But in 356 BC the temple was burned by a madman called Herostratus, who wanted to make himself famous by destroying this magnificent monument. This supposedly happened on the night Alexander the Great was born, and it was said that the goddess failed to save her temple because she was attending Alexander's birth.

The Temple Rebuilt

Work on a new temple soon began, probably under the direction of Dinocrates, Alexander the Great's architect. It was similar to the Artemisium and was built on top of its remains, but the new temple was even grander and was made entirely of marble. Marble steps surrounded the building. The high platform was 255 feet (78.5 meters) wide and 425 feet (131 meters) long. Some of the most famous artists of the time made sculptures for the temple, and it probably contained a cult statue of Artemis. The temple had 127 columns, some with decorated bases, and the triangular pediment was richly decorated with statues of Amazons, the fierce fighting women of Greek legend. This enormous building appears on many ancient coins.

Temple Life

The temple and worship of the goddess were very important in the city's life. On days of special celebrations statues of Artemis were carried through the streets in great processions, accompanied by dancers, musicians, and priests blowing horns. Silver images of the goddess were made by the city silversmiths and sold to pilgrims.

The temple was also a place of refuge, and those who sheltered there were not supposed to be harmed by their enemies. Unfortunately this was not always the case, and some people who fled there were killed.

The priests and priestesses of the temple were not allowed to marry and had to work hard; coins from ancient Ephesus show images of busy bees, the sign of the priestesses. Many people gave money to the temple and it became very rich.

A carved column base from the temple of Artemis.

A Miraculous Find

After the death of Alexander the Great in 323 BC, earth carried down by the Cayster River blocked up the harbor and the center of the city moved away from the temple. Ephesus came under Roman rule and became the wealthiest city in the Roman empire. The Romans worshiped Artemis under the name Diana, so the temple became known as the Temple of Diana.

In AD 262 Ephesus was attacked and damaged by the Goths, and Christians later allowed the temple to decay. Marble from the temple was used for buildings nearby, and the area was slowly covered by sand and soil. By the seventeenth century, Ephesus had disappeared. It was rediscovered by an Englishman, John Turtle Wood, who began excavations there in 1863. For six years he found no trace of the temple. Then he discovered an ancient notice in the theater, describing a religious procession that led from a city gate to the temple. Acting on this clue, Wood uncovered a marble road, and found the temple at the end of the road some way from the city, 20 feet (6 meters) below a swamp. Little of the temple remained above the foundations. The base and some columns were found in 1871, and two beautifully carved column bases from the temple are now in the British Museum.

"It excels all others in magnificence and splendor." *Pausanias*

Great Temples and Religious Centers

Today the remains of the city of Ephesus attract many visitors, though there is little to see of the temple apart from a few ruins. But some marvelous Greek temples and altars in other parts of the Greek world survive. The Parthenon in Athens is one of the greatest temples still standing. The splendid Altar of Zeus from the ancient city of Pergamon can now be seen in the Pergamon Museum in Berlin. The style of these monuments gives us a good idea of how the great temple complex of Artemis looked.

Great religious centers still exist today. Mecca in Saudi Arabia is a Muslim holy city. Canterbury Cathedral in England and St. Peter's in Rome are Christian centers of worship. Benares in India is a place of pilgrimage for Hindus. Jerusalem in Israel is holy for Christians, Muslims, and Jews.

Above: **Canterbury Cathedral, England.**

Below: **The ruins of Ephesus today.**

The Lighthouse of Alexandria

Alexandria in Egypt was famous throughout the ancient world as a center of learning and culture. One of its most splendid buildings was the Pharos, the first lighthouse ever built.

Alexandria was named after its founder, Alexander the Great, who was born in 356 BC in Macedon, a kingdom in the far north of Greece. His father Philip II was a great king and soldier. Alexander was only 19 when his father died, but he quickly became the most important ruler in all Greece. He conquered many other countries and created a massive empire.

One of the first kingdoms Alexander overcame was Persia, which had ruled Egypt for two centuries. The Egyptians were delighted when Alexander drove the Persians from their land, and they accepted him as their king and even as a god.

Alexander the Great.

Plan for a City

Alexander visited Egypt in 332 BC. While he was there, he decided to build a city by the sea so that ships could travel between his kingdoms in Egypt and Greece. But where should it be? On the north coast of Egypt, on the Mediterranean Sea, Alexander found a fishing village called Rhacotis, which lay on a wide harbor on the delta of the Nile River. Alexander left instructions with his architect Dinocrates for a city to be built there, and then moved on quickly to conquer other lands. Sadly, he didn't see the city that was built there because in 323 BC he died suddenly, far away in Babylon. His body was later brought back to the city and buried there in a grand tomb called the Soma, which has now disappeared.

> "When Alexander arrived and perceived
> the advantage of the situation,
> he determined to build the city
> on the (natural) harbor."
> *Strabo*

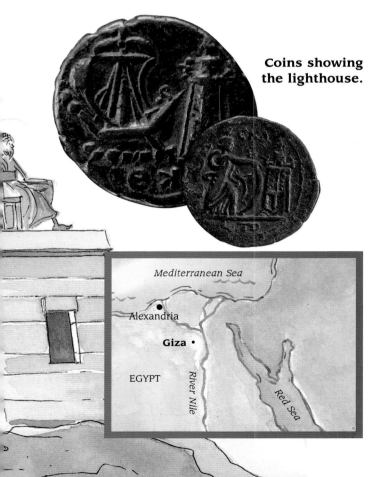

Coins showing the lighthouse.

Mediterranean Sea

Alexandria

Giza

EGYPT

River Nile

Red Sea

Building the Lighthouse

When Alexander the Great died, his friend, the general Ptolemy 1 Soter, became the ruler of Egypt. He founded a dynasty which ruled Egypt until 30 BC when its last ruler, the famous queen Cleopatra VII, died. Ptolemy at once began to build the magnificent city Alexander had imagined. The coast near Alexandria was very flat, the sea was shallow, and there were dangerous reefs nearby, so a lighthouse was built to help sailors find their way to the city safely.

It seems likely that the lighthouse was begun by Ptolemy I Soter but finished some twelve years later, probably around 280 BC, by his successor, Ptolemy II Philadelphus. It was built on a small rocky island near the coast. The island was called the Pharos and the lighthouse was often called the Pharos as well. It was believed that it was paid for by Sostratos of Cnidus, who dedicated it to the gods for the protection of sailors.

A Towering Monument

No one knows exactly what the lighthouse looked like, but it was shown on ancient coins, mosaics, and other objects, and recent excavations at Alexandria have revealed more. Travelers who visited Alexandria also described the lighthouse. It was a gigantic building which stood about 385 feet (117 meters) high. Although it was built of limestone, some parts of it may have been covered by white marble. It had three storys and tapered upward to the top.

The first and largest part of the building was square, the next stage was octagonal, and the third level was circular. There were many rooms within the square base to house the people who worked in the lighthouse and to store materials. A sloping ramp led from the ground to the lighthouse door. Inside, a ramp and then a staircase led up to the top of the building. On its top stood a statue of the Greek god Zeus. It is possible that other statues decorated the building too.

21

A Glorious City

The city of Alexandria flourished under the Ptolemies. From the time it was founded in 332 BC until it was overcome by the Arabs in AD 642 it was the capital of Egypt and many famous people lived there. The last of the Ptolemies, Cleopatra VII, was a woman of great charm and intelligence, and she became one of the most famous queens in history.

Coin showing Cleopatra VII.

Apart from the lighthouse, Alexandria was also known for its great library, the largest in the ancient world, which contained over 500,000 documents. Scholars from all over the ancient world, such as the mathematician Archimedes, came to study here and it became a brilliant center of learning and trade.

"Its purpose is to provide a beacon for the ships sailing by night to warn them of shallows and to mark the entrance to the harbor."
Pliny the Elder

The Light

Almost nothing is known about how the lighthouse worked. Light may have been provided by a fire at the bottom of the building, and this light was probably magnified by a reflection on mirrors of polished metal at the top. In later centuries some artists showed a beacon fire on the top of the building. The light could be seen far out to sea.

A Long Life

The lighthouse was used for more than 1,000 years. It was very strongly built—few buildings have served their purpose for as long—and it provided light for sailors for more than 17 centuries.

In AD 956 and again in 1303 and 1323 the lighthouse was badly damaged by earthquakes. A visitor to Alexandria reported in 1326 and 1349 that it was ruined. In the fifteenth century the Arabs built a fort called the Fort of Kait Bey on the site of the lighthouse, and the island where the Fort stands is now joined to the mainland. The fort can still be visited today, and so the memory of the lighthouse lives on. It is still associated with Alexandria just as New York is known for the Statue of Liberty and Athens for the Parthenon.

The Fort of Kait Bey.

A Wondrous Model

The lighthouse soon became a model for others. The Romans copied its design and built several lighthouses, including one in Ostia, a port near Rome. Over the next 2,000 years lighthouses were built all over the world. Their light was provided by fire until medieval times, after which oil burners were used. Today, most lighthouses are powered by electricity, gas, or the sun. These technological advances meant that lighthouse keepers no longer had to live in the lighthouses all the time to tend the lights, so they could be built in very isolated places.

The Pharos was also said to be a model for the shape of the minarets in Muslim mosques.

Left: **The Tower of Hercules, a recontructed Roman lighthouse at Coruna, Spain.**

Decline and Rediscovery

After the death of Cleopatra, Egypt was seized by the Romans and then by the Arabs. The new Arab rulers built another capital city called Cairo to the south, and Alexandria fell into decline. Then in the nineteenth century it became a busy trading center again, and today it is the second-largest city in Egypt.

Much of the ancient city of Alexandria disappeared under the sea after earthquakes. In the 1960s archaeologists started to explore under the sea near the city and in the harbor, and near the Fort of Kait Bey divers found massive blocks and statues which they believe may have formed part of the lighthouse. Some of the blocks, which weigh up to 40 tons, have been pulled out of the sea. The remains of a palace and a temple have also been discovered underwater in the harbor. Archaeologists hope that more exciting discoveries will be made.

An underwater archaeologist at work in Alexandria harbor.

The Mausoleum of Halicarnassus

The Mausoleum—the tomb of Maussollos, the king of Caria—was colossal in size and was sumptuously decorated with many statues. It was one of the world's most splendid tombs and became so famous that the word "mausoleum" is now used to describe all large tombs.

In the fourth century BC, the kingdom of Caria in Asia Minor (modern Turkey) was part of the Persian empire. Maussollos ruled Caria for the Persians from 377 to 353 BC. As he became more powerful and independent, he decided to create a magnificent new center for his kingdom. He moved his capital from Mylasa, a city in the hills, to Halicarnassus, which lay by the sea. Today the city is called Bodrum.

Maussollos turned Halicarnassus into a gleaming city with many grand buildings, but the most memorable of them all was his own tomb, which he began to build during his lifetime. Work was continued after his death by his wife Artemisia who, in accordance with local custom, was also Maussollos's sister. Artemisia ruled Caria after Maussollos's death, but two years later she also died. The tomb was finished after her death, probably around 350 BC.

> "These sculptors in particular made the Mausoleum one of the Seven Wonders of the World."
> *Pliny the Elder*

The Delight of Its Age

The tomb became known for its great architectural beauty and its sculptural decoration. Pliny the Elder and the ancient architect and engineer Vitruvius tell us that the greatest sculptors of the time worked on it, including Bryaxis, Leochares, Timotheos, and Skopas. It was said that each one of them designed the decoration of one side of the tomb. It is possible that a local man called Satyrus supervised the whole of this vast building project.

Groups of sculptures lined the base of the tomb and single statues stood between the columns on the colonnade. On the top was the tomb's crowning glory, a colossal statue of a four-horse chariot. Giant statues of Maussollos and his wife may have stood inside the chariot or lower down on the tomb. There were also huge statues of lions and of people who may have been members of Maussollos's court. The statues were painted with bright colors and fragments of the paint still survive on their remains.

Elaborate carved panels, called reliefs, also decorated the Mausoleum. They showed chariot races and fierce battles between Greeks and Amazons, Lapiths, and Centaurs.

These huge statues from the Mausoleum may be Maussollos and Artemisia.

25

A Spectacular Tomb

Maussollos's tomb was built in the heart of the city, high on the hill overlooking the harbor. It was a combination of different styles—Greek, local Carian, and some Egyptian. In the first century AD Pliny the Elder visited the tomb and described how it looked.

The tomb was made up of three main parts, he said. Its massive rectangular base, the podium, was about 120 feet (36.5 meters) by 100 feet (30.4 meters). The podium supported a colonnade or row of 36 columns in a style known as "Ionic" which was used in much Greek architecture. You can recognize Ionic columns by the scroll decoration at the top. Above this was a pyramid of 24 marble steps. Underground, inside the tomb, was a burial chamber with a coffin of white alabaster and gold. The entire tomb stood a massive 140 feet (42.5 meters) high.

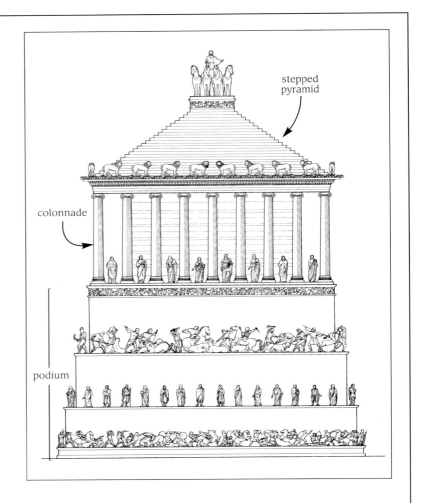

stepped pyramid

colonnade

podium

A Monument Destroyed

The Mausoleum stood for many centuries, but then, in the thirteenth century, it was badly shaken by an earthquake. More trouble was in store. The Knights of St. John of Malta arrived in Halicarnassus and built the castle of St. Peter in the town in 1402. When they strengthened the castle in 1494 they used some of the stone from the tomb and over the following years they took more. White marble from the tomb was ground up to make the mortar used to cement together the stones of the castle. Even the tomb's burial chamber was plundered. The knights also took some of the tomb's beautiful reliefs and built them into the castle walls for decoration.

By 1522, little of Maussollos's magnificent tomb remained and all that is left today are the

Relief of Amazons fighting Greeks from the Mausoleum. The relief is now in the British Museum.

foundations and some broken columns. But in 1846 some of the decorative reliefs from the castle were removed and sent to the British Museum.

Finding Extraordinary Remains

In 1856 the Englishman Charles Newton began excavating the site. At first he found little. Then in a field he discovered steps, the Mausoleum's foundation wall, and parts of giant statues, which must have fallen down in the earthquake. Fortunately they were covered with soil so they were not destroyed by the Knights of St. John. Sixty-six statues and fragments were found, and these are now in the British Museum. They include parts of a great statue of a horse, lions, parts of the reliefs, and colossal statues of a man and woman. The statues look very lifelike and seem to represent real people. They show just how lavishly the tomb was decorated.

Between 1966 and 1977 the Danish archaeologist Professor Kristian Jeppersen uncovered the foundations of the Mausoleum and explored the tomb chamber. He found that Maussollos had been buried with offerings for the dead, as was the custom in the area. The remains of sheep, calves, chickens, a goose, and eggs were found. Even as late as 1975, more parts of the reliefs were found nearby.

This stone lion and horse with a bronze bridle come from the Mausoleum.

Great Tombs

The Great Pyramid of Khufu and the Mausoleum were two of the greatest tombs of the ancient world. But throughout history and up until our own times, other great tombs have been built. Like the Mausoleum, some were planned by rulers to keep their memories alive. In Roman times the emperor Augustus was buried in a grand tomb on the Campus Martius which can still be seen near the Church of Saint Roche in Rome.

Others were built out of great love. One of the world's most beautiful tombs is the Taj Mahal in Agra in India. This was built between 1631 and 1653 by the Indian emperor Shah Jahan in memory of his wife.

The Taj Mahal.

27

The Colossus of Rhodes

In 282 BC the people of the island of Rhodes completed a gigantic statue, the Colossus, to celebrate their victory over an enemy. It overlooked the entrance to their harbor and was the largest statue ever made in the ancient world.

GREECE

TURKEY

• Ephesus

• Halicarnassus

Olympia

• **Rhodes**

Mediterranean Sea

Coin showing Helios, the sun god.

Many thousands of years ago groups of ancient Greek people settled on Rhodes, a small, fertile island in the Mediterranean Sea near the coast of Asia Minor. In 408 BC the islanders built the city of Rhodes, in the northeast of the island, as their capital. Rhodes became the richest city-state in the Greek world. It had wide streets, fine walls, a temple, and many statues and was known for its artists and scholars. Rhodes also had a large navy.

In 305 BC some enemies of Rhodes besieged the city. The Rhodians fought them off bravely, and after a year they triumphed. The siege was lifted, the enemies were driven away, and the city was saved.

A Great Celebration

The Rhodians were overjoyed. To celebrate their victory, they sold the valuable siege equipment their enemies left behind and used the money to build a great statue of the sun god Helios, the city's protector.

Chares, a citizen of the island, was the sculptor chosen to make the statue and it took him 12 years, from 294 to 282 BC, to create his masterpiece. The statue became known as the "Colossus," an Asiatic word meaning "statue." From the time of the Colossus of Rhodes, the word "colossus" was only used to mean gigantic statues.

We do not know where the Colossus stood or exactly what it looked like. It is mentioned many times by ancient authors, but most do not give very detailed information. We do know that it stood a towering 110 feet (33 meters) high and may have shown Helios standing with a torch in one hand and perhaps a spear in the other.

> "...he created, with incredible boldness, a god similar to the real God; for he gave a second Sun to the world."
> *Philo of Byzantium*

The Site of the Statue

People in medieval times had some very romantic ideas about the Colossus. They believed that it had straddled the entrance to the harbor of Rhodes with one foot placed on each shore so that ships sailed into the harbor under the statue, between its feet. This is unlikely to be true—even the Colossus wasn't big enough to stand right across the harbor entrance. Most probably, the statue stood further into the town or at the side of the harbor, where Fort St. Nicolas now stands.

This sixteenth-century engraving shows the Colossus standing astride the harbor.

The Statue Vanishes

The Colossus of Rhodes did not stand for long. In 226 BC, only 56 years after it was finished, a violent earthquake shook Rhodes, and the statue crashed to the ground. It is said that it was broken at the knees. King Ptolemy of Egypt offered to help repair the statue, but the Rhodians were warned by a prophecy that it should not be restored. Three centuries later, Pliny the Elder saw it lying on the rocks. For nearly 900 years, the Colossus stayed where it had fallen.

Building the Statue

The statue was so big that its creation was an incredible feat of technology. Chares's workmanship won great admiration. Nobody knows for sure how the statue was built, but the drawing below shows the most

Rhodes harbor today.

likely method. Modern archaeologists believe that Chares began by making a base of white marble, then built a frame of iron on the base. The legs and the lower body of the statue were made of bronze and fitted into place on the frame. Then the hollow bronze shape was filled with stone for balance. The finished parts of the statue were covered with earth so that the workmen could stand on it to add on the rest of the parts. When the bronze statue was completely finished the earth was taken away.

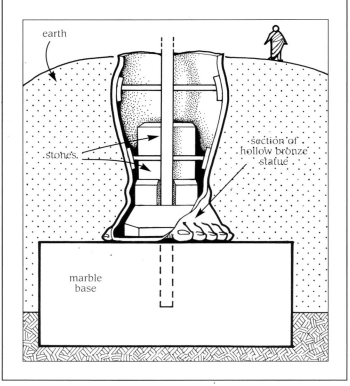

earth

stones

section of hollow bronze statue

marble base

Rhodes was damaged by disastrous earthquakes in AD 345 and 515, and the city's fortunes declined. Then in AD 654 the Arabs overwhelmed Rhodes. Soon afterward they sold the remaining pieces of the Colossus to a Jewish trader from Emesa as scrap metal. It is said that he took the pieces to Syria, and that 900 camels were needed to carry them.

Who knows what became of this fabulous statue after that? The island was later ruled by the Knights of St John of Malta, a group of medieval Christian soldiers. They rebuilt the city of Rhodes, and it prospered again, but by then even the place where the statue had stood was forgotten.

The Statue's Legacy

The word "colossus" has come to be used for many giant statues, and the statue itself inspired others. In Roman times it became popular to build great statues at the entrance to harbors, and this tradition has continued into modern times. In 1886 the Statue of Liberty was erected in the harbor of New York City. It stands 152 feet (46 meters) high. The sculptor, a Frenchman called Auguste Bartholdi, was influenced by the Colossus of Rhodes. Like its ancient model, the Statue of Liberty is a symbol of freedom.

"Even lying on the ground it is amazing." Pliny the Elder

Ancient Writers

Much of what we know about the Seven Wonders comes from ancient travelers and writers, who saw or heard about the Wonders. You can read some of their words in the pages of this book.

Herodotus was a Greek who was born in Halicarnassus in Asia Minor (modern Turkey) between 490 and 480 BC and died in 425 BC. The Romans called him "the Father of History." He was an adventurous traveler who visited many countries and wrote a book about the war between the Greeks and the Persians called *The Histories*. It was the first history book to be written in the Western world. In it Herodotus described the countries he had visited, including Egypt and Babylonia.

Another writer was **Philo of Byzantium**, an engineer who lived around 250 BC. Little is known about him but he wrote a work called *The Seven Sights of the World* which became very popular.

Diodorus of Sicily was a Greek historian, who lived in the first century BC and wrote an entire history of the world down to his own day.

Another Greek historian of the first century was **Strabo** (64 BC–AD 21), who was born in Amaseia on the Black Sea. Strabo travelled widely and wrote a book called *The Geography* which described the countries, cities, and famous people of the world.

Marcus Vitruvius Pollio, known as **Vitruvius**, lived in the first century BC and became an important architect and engineer in Rome, where he looked after the military engines and managed the city's water supply. Vitruvius wrote *The Ten Books of Architecture*, the world's first book on the subject. Many famous artists and architects, such as Michelangelo, studied this work.

Pliny the Elder, whose real name was Gaius Plinius Secundus, was born around AD 23. Pliny held important positions in the Roman government and also wrote many books, one of which was called *Natural History*. This book contains much information about scientific and artistic activities. Pliny's curiosity led to his death. When the volcano Vesuvius erupted violently near Pompeii in Southern Italy in AD 79, Pliny sailed across the Bay of Naples to get a good view and was killed.

In the second century AD, **Pausanius**, a Greek doctor from Asia Minor, went on a long journey through Greece. He studied the places he visited carefully and wrote a book called *Guide to Greece*, which describes in detail the buildings and monuments he saw.

The exciting accounts of the Seven Wonders left by these writers helped keep the memory of the monuments alive. Many—but not all—of the things they wrote have now been proved true by archaeologists.

Index

Picture Credits

Sarah Warburton drew the illustrations and maps on pp. 3, 4–5, 7, 8, 9, 12–13, 14, 16–17, 20–21, 24–25, 28 and on the front cover.

All photographs were taken by The British Museum Photography and Imaging Department, © The British Museum, apart from the following:

p. 5 – Robert Partridge: The Ancient Egyptian Picture Library
p. 6 – Photograph by Graham Harrison, © The British Museum
p. 7 (left) – Delia Pemberton; (right) – © Photo RMN; (background) – Photograph by Graham Harrison, © The British Museum
p. 10 (top) – Ny Carlsberg Glyptotek © Ole Haupt
p. 11 (top and bottom left) – Deutches Archäologisches Institut, Athens; (top right) – Representation Plus; (middle right) – Allsport UK Ltd; (bottom right) – © National Tourist Organization of Greece
p. 13 – Bildarchiv Preußischer Kulturbesitz

p. 15 (top) – Amministrazione Isole Borromeo srl; (background) – Anne Searight
p. 17 (top) – Turkish Tourist Board; (bottom) – Ian Jenkins
p. 18 (top) – Peter Clayton
p. 19 (top) – Dean and Chapter of Canterbury; (background) – Sam Moorhead
p. 22 (middle) – Bridgeman Art Library; (bottom) – Diana Bentley
p. 23 (top) – Spanish Tourist Office; (background) – S. Compoint/Corbis Sygma
p. 27 (right) – Michael O'Flynn
p. 29 – Peter Clayton
p. 30 (top) – National Tourist Board of Greece; (bottom left) – drawing by Susan Bird; (bottom right) – NYCVB/London